# Neural Age

John A Drakopoulos

# Neural Age

John A Drakopoulos received his PhD for Stanford University in 1995. He has been a professor and a research scientist in major corporations as well as a few startups. His work has often surpassed the state-of-the-art. He has been working with neural networks and he has been a strong advocate for neural network research and applications for nearly three decades.

# Acknowledgment

The author would like to thank Heather Alden and Gordon Rios for reading the first manuscript and for their many helpful comments and suggestions

# Table of Contents

# Prologue

Computers and technology have dramatically changed our way of life. Our world is now immersed in computing. Computer science is the primary scientific field that has effected those changes. However, there has been an extraordinary prejudice in the field that has taken precedence over facts and scientific rigor. It has hindered progress and it has led us to a constructivist predicament.

All this may be hard to believe given the many successes of the field and the lucrative industry behind it. Yet, upon closer examination, things are not as they appear. The history and the treatment of artificial neural networks provide sufficient evidence and a clear verdict, the tangle of thorns so preposterous that, in comparison, even the Carrollian queen may appear rational and inoffensive: "Sentence first -- verdict afterwards."

After many decades, a different perspective and a paradigm shift are finally developing in the Wonderland. A new era has begun. Throughout this century, neural networks will redefine most of computer science. They will transform and improve art, science, and society. Most aspects of human activity and intellect will be affected. Manufacturing, construction, and engineering; finance, security, and defense; travel, transportation, and agriculture; politics, arts, education, and entertainment; biology, medicine and many other fields of science; they will all change.

However, in order to imagine the future, we must first understand the past and how we arrived at the present state. We will present the evidence in three main exhibits.

Chapter 1 is the first exhibit and it is a brief history of neural networks. Chapter 2 is the second exhibit and it is about a constructivist bias that has dominated the software industry. Chapter 3 is about an anti-neural prejudice in computer science and it is the third and final exhibit. The three exhibits raise some important questions and provide evidence and answers as well. Chapter 4 defines intelligence formally and examines the relationship between learning and intelligence. (Previous definitions of intelligence are abstract and qualitative.) Chapter 5 considers a number of current applications of neural networks and discusses their potential growth and extensions. Finally, chapters 6 and 7 depart from scientific discourse and focus more on speculation as they try to imagine the future of neural networks and the changes that they may effect to the world in the course of the 21st century.

Chapters 1 to 4 are expository but they also contain a considerable amount of technical information. We thus recommend that readers outside the field start at chapter 5 and proceed to the end; then return to chapters 2 and 3 and finally to chapters 1 and 4.

Now, let us proceed with the three exhibits.

# 1. The rise of neural networks

A diverse scientific and entrepreneurial enterprise is currently underway. Various elaborate terms have been used for it, such as "a revolution", "the new electricity", or "a tsunami". Others prefer more 'scientific' terms such as data science or artificial intelligence. Despite the connotations and the long history of failures, the latter is a term that currently resonates with entrepreneurs and government agencies and excites the public imagination. Others use more technical terms such as big data, machine learning, or the latest buzzword: deep learning.

In this book, we will refer to the above enterprise as neural networks. We consider that to be the true and most accurate name of it. We dropped the term 'artificial' because we would like to focus on the underlying universal mathematical models rather than their implementation or their relationship with biological intelligence.

In its most common form, a *neural network* is a simple but fundamental mathematical construction. It is a composition of alternating polynomial and non-polynomial functions. This is often visualized as a sequence of *layers*, each layer representing a pair of polynomial and non-polynomial functions. The first layer is used to denote the input to the net and the last to produce the output. The rest of the layers are indicated as *hidden*. The *depth* of the network is defined to be to be the number of layers (which is the number of hidden layers plus two for the input and output layers.) *Deep neural networks* are simply networks with large depth. Information usually flows from one layer to subsequent layers only; and it that case, the network is called *feed-forward*.

# 1. The rise of neural networks

A feed-forward neural network (FNN) is a composition of alternating polynomial ($\Sigma$) and non-polynomial ($\phi$) functions.

A convolutional neural network (CNN) is an FNN with one or more iterative polynomial transformations.

A recurrent neural network (RNN) is an FNN with one or more backward connections.

A recurrent convolutional neural network (RCNN) is both convolutional and recurrent.

**Figure 1.** Common neural network types

The polynomial functions are usually linear or quadratic. When one or more of the linear functions are actually smaller transformations that are iteratively applied across shifting parts of their input, the network is called *convolutional*. When some of the inputs to one layer come from subsequent layer(s), the network is called *recurrent*. And when a network is both

4

convolutional and recurrent, it is called *convolutional recurrent*. Figure 1 shows those types of neural networks.

The non-polynomial functions are usually simple functions such as sigmoid, Gaussian, rectifier functions etc. In recurrent networks, more complex functions are used such as gated recurrent or long short-term memory units. Those implement a linearly parameterized recursion with or without latent variables, respectively.

(In general, we must impose a restriction that the polynomial functions are not fixed and equal to the identity function except in special cases -- otherwise everything can be represented as a neural network. An example of a special case is a soft-max layer, which is a layer that emphasizes the maximum of all its values at the expense of the other values. In such a layer, the polynomial transformation is indeed fixed and equal to the identity function and the non-polynomial one is a rational function.)

Given the above definitions, it should be clear that neural networks are elementary mathematical constructions.

Computationally, none of the above structures are novel. A feed-forward network is the neural equivalent of a sequence of instructions while convolution and recurrence are the neural versions of iterations (a.k.a. loops) and recursion, respectively. The novelty, if any, is in the learning part. In a traditional computation model, a human has to provide the code for the body of the loops and the (recursive) functions. With neural networks, one only provides the computational mechanisms (sequence, iteration, recursion) and the network learns its function(s) from the data. In a sense, a neural network generates its own code, extracting it from the data. (There are various approaches that enable networks to learn their structure too but those are beyond the scope of this book.)

# 1. The rise of neural networks

Learning is not a novel approach or paradigm. Rudimentary learning forms, such as linear models, were introduced many decades ago and they precede most of computer science. For example, Fisher's linear discriminant was published in 1936 and the perceptron algorithm was invented in 1957. Back-propagation, which is simply a gradient descent method to train multi-layer neural networks, was published in 1986 while variants or less generic versions of it were published throughout the 1960s, 1970s, and early 1980s. Convolutional neural networks were introduced in the 1980s and were inspired by earlier work on biological processes and the organization of the animal visual cortex, such as the work on receptive fields by Hubel and Wiesel in the 1950s and 1960s, their seminal publication in 1968. Recurrent neural networks were also introduced in the 1980s. The Hopfield network is one of the earliest types, first described in 1974 and popularized in 1982.

There are multiple forms of learning. An important distinction is between *supervised* and *unsupervised* learning. In the former, the learned function is inferred from labeled training data (a 'supervising' agent or process provides the labels). In the latter case, there are no labels in the data and the learner must infer its function from distributional or structural characteristics of the training data. Supervised learning can address considerably more specific and complex tasks but its main limitation is the size of the training set. This is the main advantage of unsupervised learning: the size of the training set is practically unlimited.

In general, learning algorithms must solve a *credit assignment problem*, that is to apply a reward or a penalty to learned parameters or factors that affect an outcome. The problem becomes harder as the (temporal, spatial, structural) distance between the outcome and the factor increases. This problem with recurrent or deep neural networks was identified and solved (to a large extent) in 1990s.

*Sparse features* are features in a domain that are absent from most samples of the domain. If we represent those features as a vector where the number zero is used to indicate absence, the vector will contain mostly zeros and will thus be numerically sparse. Words are a common (and essential) example of sparse features. If the domain is documents, only a small percentage of all words will be present in each document.

Sparse features represent an acute problem for neural networks -- and learning in general. If we were to train a neural network in the standard supervised way using sparse features, a labeled training set of extraordinary size would be required. This is an important limitation because words are an essential component of natural language.

An elegant solution to the above problem was proposed in 2003. The idea is to use the hidden state of a neural network to represent words (or combinations of words or characters). The initial network is trained in an unsupervised manner to distinguish between actual documents (such as articles in news corpora) and random sequences of words or characters. This initial and unsupervised preprocessing is then used to map words to numeric vectors that are derived from the hidden state of the network. The vectors are usually called *embeddings* because the hidden state of such networks is an embedding of a high-dimension space to a lower-dimension space. The high-dimension space contains one dimension for each distinct word (or character sequence) and the low-dimension space contains one dimension for each hidden unit in the network. Distinct words can easily be more than 100,000 while only few hundred hidden units are usually used for such embedding networks. Figure 2 shows a projection of embeddings in two dimensions.

The unsupervised form of the above step allows us to use data sets that are sufficiently large to handle the sparsity of words. Such embeddings usually preserve semantic similarities and relations between words. (For example, the embedding of the

**Figure 2.** Word embeddings projected in two dimensions. (Source: ruder.io.)

word "queen" is similar to the embedding of the word "king" minus the embedding of the word "man" plus the embedding of the word "woman".)

In a sense, the embeddings have achieved a very important milestone. For the first time in the history of computer science, we can legitimately claim that computers have developed a form of understanding of words and perhaps human language. It is certainly an elementary form but it is a form of understanding nevertheless. More importantly, it is a form of understanding that was not engineered by humans into computers but was extracted from data using learning.

Of course, a sufficiently large labeled training set could be generated using crowd-sourcing or the great financial resources of governments or corporations. Such a crowd-sourcing approach has been used for images with the Imagenet project. Images are labeled by humans to indicate the pictured objects. The Wordnet data base, which is a large lexical database of English, is used to organize the labels and the images.

The approach is valid and perhaps necessary, if the goal is to create a link between vision and human language, associating words with their visual representations. However, it is not as valid or necessary if the goal is to recognize specific objects in scenes or develop generic vision that is capable of recognizing objects but does not map them to descriptions (most animals have no sounds or other descriptions for most of the objects they see.) And, of course, the usual trade-off of supervised vs. unsupervised learning apply for the two methods.

The above developments are the primary foundational blocks behind current neural network enterprise. One important milestone was the superior performance of a convolutional neural network on the Imagenet database in 2012. Another important milestone was the combination of word embeddings and convolutional neural networks that achieved state-of-the-art results in a number of natural language processing tasks in 2011. Those results were no surprise for a minority of experts who truly understood the extraordinary potential of neural networks. However, they were critical in setting the stage for the current enterprise. The interest and emphasis in neural networks increased dramatically in subsequent years. Results started pouring in for various domains and applications. Even fields such as speech recognition, effectively stagnant for more than a decade, experienced large gains with neural networks. And some experts started declaring metaphorical revolutions and tsunamis.

# 1. The rise of neural networks

Exhibit number one is the above brief history and exposition of neural networks. It raises crucial questions. The mathematical developments are relatively simple, and yet they took an excessive amount of time to be established. It took almost thirty years from the discovery of the perceptron algorithm to the introduction of back-propagation. It took two decades from the discovery of receptive fields to convolutional neural networks. It took three more decades before convolutional neural networks were combined with embeddings. The embeddings were introduced in 2003 and yet it took nearly a decade for their potential to be realized. Overall, it took more than fifty years from the perceptron to the current enterprise. In comparison, if quantum physics were as inefficient a paradigm as neural networks, it would probably have taken one more century to achieve the current level of mathematical sophistication. This leads to the first question: why are neural networks such an inefficient paradigm? Another related question is the timing: why is the neural enterprise taking place now? The latter is a popular topic in on-line discussions and forums, surrounded by various myths and fallacies.

We will attempt to answer the above questions as well as dispel the myths with exhibit number three, which incidentally appears in section three of this book. However, we must now proceed with exhibit number two.

## 2. The epidemic of constructivism

Constructivism is essentially a rejection of autonomy. As an artistic and architectural philosophy, it originated in Russia circa 1913 and it was a rejection of autonomous art. Similarly, in science and engineering, constructivism postulates the existence or even the necessity of creators (usually scientists or engineers). Inevitably, the output of a constructivist process is limited by the ability of its postulated agents.

Constructivism has been virtually omnipresent in engineering, its success primarily based on human ingenuity. However, there are limitations to human intellect as there are limitations to any computation, their most elementary form derives from the hierarchy of computational complexity. In computer science, and particularly in software engineering, constructivism has been taken to a new extreme that seems to defy or deny the existence of such limitations. Let us examine this condition in more detail.

Modern operating systems contain well above fifty million lines of source code. This is an astonishing number. Even if an engineer was able to produce one thousand lines of code per day and maintain that rate 365 days a year, they would need about 137 years just to author the code. If we make more reasonable assumptions, such as 200 lines per day, 5 days a week, and 48 work weeks per year, the above estimate is revised to 1042 years. Those estimates do not include testing, debugging, performance monitoring, or any quality assurance. In reality, the amount of time to test, monitor, and debug the code often exceeds the time to design and produce the first version. We should also add communication overhead and redundancy into the equation, if more than one engineer is to implement the project. And of course there is the cost of maintaining the code. If we add all those together, we would end up with an estimate of multi-thousand person-years to implement such large code. Consequently, if such a project is to be designed and implemented in the course of few years, thousands of employees are required.

The above numbers have unfortunate if not dire consequences. They are not exclusive to operating systems either. Other complex systems such as search engines or databases consist of many millions of lines of source code. One might wonder how it is possible for humans to engineer projects at such scale. The short answer is negative. Those projects and their products can hardly be classified as engineering. Engineers and managers often admit that the code is simply a 'mess' that needs to be re-factored, re-written, or re-designed. The latter is ironic because the code was not truly designed on the first place.

When thousands of engineers are involved in a single multi-million-line project, each one is responsible for a tiny part of it. Each engineer or manager has a very limited understanding and range in the project. The vast majority of the code is effectively and inevitably treated as a black box. Engineers or managers would never read or even access most of the code. They cannot possibly read millions of lines of code or even high level descriptions of it in the course of their residence with the project. The temporal nature of employment only aggravates the problem. Employees may move on with other responsibilities or career opportunities, often changing employers, and their replacements have to start from scratch in their effort to understand the code.

In this book, we use the term *over-partitioning* to refer to projects that are partitioned in as many parts as to make comprehensive definitions and understanding practically impossible. We consider projects that must be over-partitioned (e.g. because of their size or complexity) to be an engineering liability.

The net effect of over-partitioning is that no one has a comprehensive view of the project and its complexity. No one can guarantee that functions, libraries, or other parts of the system are appropriately used. No one is aware of all the interactions of the components of the system. No one can even name all the components or some significant percentage of them. As the size of the code grows, dynamic and often chaotic patterns settle in. Engineers gradually accept that the code is an enormous black box that contains large numbers of glitches and vulnerabilities. In order to deal with those, the software industry constantly patches up their code issuing regular and often urgent updates. This is so common nowadays that it is no longer considered worth to be mentioned in the news. Consumers have been conditioned (if not forced) to accept such low quality products. And they pay premium prices for them that factor in the excessive engineering cost.

The above is neither evidence of engineering mediocrity nor an elaborate scheme to create monopolies and costly products that are prohibitively expensive to reproduce. At large scale, constructivism necessitates over-partitioning and thus becomes the source of the problem. The latter fact is part of exhibit number two. There is an extraordinary degree of prejudice in computer science; and that prejudice has led the software industry and has pushed constructivism well beyond its breaking point.

Let us consider an example. Few decades ago, in a major software corporation, a project started to replace the code of one of their main products because of quality issues and concerns. Much to their credit, the involved employees were honest enough to admit the problem and they sought a solution. The company decided to keep the old code around and maintain it until the new code was ready to replace it. It proved to be a prudent decision. For the new code turned out to be more problematic than the original and the new project was simply abandoned. It was not an incidental failure. Because of its sheer size, the quality of the code will always be minimal no matter how many times teams implement it. The software industry has clearly exceeded the human limits.

There have been legitimate efforts and paradigms to push the limits of human software engineering. For example, object oriented programming is such a paradigm and it has had a pronounced effect. Open source is a mode of development that greatly improves software quality. However, in the end, all of those efforts merely translate the limits and they only postpone the inevitable.

In the long term, constructivism is strictly ephemeral because it cannot scale up. Metaphorically, it is a guest in computer science -- as well as any science or engineering that aspires to address structural complexities of arbitrary scale; and it has already overstayed its welcome.

The excessive emphasis on constructivism has also eroded style and aesthetics. Long gone is the elegance and brevity of formalisms and systems such as the C programming language or the Unix operating system. Modern systems are rather elaborate, verbose, overwrought, and often cumbersome. This is no surprise. The ability of humans to create well-designed systems reduces with the complexity of the system. After certain levels, human capacity is exhausted and designs and engineering yield to various necessities and redundancies. Indeed, when teams struggle to make a system work on the first place without embarrassing glitches and vulnerabilities, elegance and aesthetics simply become a luxury.

At this point, we should note that many scientists and mathematicians consider algorithms and computer programming as one of the most striking and beautiful areas of science and mathematics. It is a rational consideration and perspective. There is rigor, brevity, and elegance in the field. There are remarkable mathematical contributions such as complexity theory, numerical computing and optimization, parsing theory or relational algebras -- just to name a few. Ingenious efficient solutions have been found for many problems. Some algorithms, like the number field sieve for example, are marvels of mathematical sophistication. However, computer programming is not the same as software engineering. The latter is more concerned with scale, maintenance, modularity, usability, documentation and many other aspects of code rather than finding efficient and ingenious solutions to problems. Constructivism is an excellent paradigm for algorithms and programming but, inevitably, a bias and a liability for large-scale engineering.

We will re-examine this state of affairs in chapter three, where we will try to explain some of the main sources of the constructivist bias and the related forces that led to it. In the remaining of this chapter, we will consider a second example, focusing on organization rather than scale.

Let us consider databases. With the current technology, and in order to create a database, one must first provide a *schema*, which is a set of formulas (*integrity constraints*) that specify the facts that can enter the database and their form. Then the entire database is built around the schema. This has all the disadvantages of *waterfall models.* Those are defined as sequential processes where information flows easily in one direction -- down like in a waterfall -- but not in the other. Upward changes, such as those that may emerge as feedback from the implementation phase or the use of the system to the design are very costly and hard or impossible to implement without a re-design. Indeed, changing the schema of a database after the database has been in operation for a while usually involves significant re-engineering. This is even worse with distributed databases where a partitioning predicate is used for physically allocating data to various storage devices or servers.

# Chapter 2. The epidemic of constructivism

Now, let us compare this with human memory. If our brains used a similar database structure then newborn children would have to predefine the form and structure of all the potential memories that could be stored in their brains before they even have any memories. If we consider that to be an absurd proposition, so we must deem the current database technology to be.

The main reason that such cumbersome technologies have been adopted in computer science is again the bias with constructivism in the field. The bias has reached such levels that it currently amounts to short-sightedness, obsession, or prejudice depending on the specific areas. Bias can be a formidable force when it points to the right direction; but it can limit us and deprive us of vision and even rationality when it reduces to a fallacy.

If the emphasis in computer science were on learning and autonomy instead of constructivism, databases would be built in a very different fashion. Data would enter an initially empty database in the form of associations between various items. Then those associations would be constantly or periodically re-organized and re-indexed based on their frequency and short-term and long-term usage. This is what seems to happen in human brains. Studies have shown that memories are re-organized during sleep to minimize the cost and energy consumption for their retrieval.

Even if we accept the current database technology as a substrate, it is not hard to train a neural network to re-organize and re-index the database based on its use. Furthermore, for databases that require lossless retrieval, it is rather inefficient to use neural connections to store the associations. A hybrid approach with external memory that is managed by a neural network would probably work best. The dynamic neural computer is such a hybrid example. (Mathematically, it is unnecessarily convoluted but it is a step in the right direction for hybrid systems.) Yet, all of this potential remains unexplored for it lies beyond the limited horizon of constructivism. The associated bias has indeed deprived adopting researchers from vision and rationality.

The above is the second part and the conclusion of exhibit number two, hereby called the *epidemic of constructivism.*

# 3. Anti-neural prejudice

Let us now proceed with exhibit number three.

In computer science, and in particular in the field of artificial intelligence, there has been an extraordinary degree of hostility and prejudice against neural networks. The exact origins of it are hard to pinpoint. It seems to have started in the late 1950s and early 1960s as a feud with heated quarrels in academic conferences. It reached a critical (and infectious) point with the publication of a deleterious book titled "Perceptrons: an introduction to computational geometry" in 1969.

There is hardly any meaningful scientific contribution in the above book. A central result -- that a linear function could not model a non-monotonic function -- is trivial and it was well-known for centuries. (Pierre Fermat was among the first mathematicians who understood the importance and the relation of monotonicity and local extrema.) Let us demonstrate the exceptional triviality of it.

**Proposition.** If $P(a,b)$ and $X(a,b)$ are a perceptron and the exclusive-or function with binary inputs $a$, $b$, respectively, then $P(a,b)$ cannot be equal to $X(a,b)$, for all $a$, $b$.

*Proof.* $P(0,b)$ and $P(1,b)$ are functions of $b$ with the same monotonicity. However, $X(0,b)$ and $X(1,b)$ are an increasing and a decreasing function of $b$, respectively.

The result is indeed so trivial that its proof is shorter than the proposition. The elaborate proof that appeared in the book can only raise questions about the authors and may suggest pretensions of a discovery. The underlying monotonicity facts are as trivial and they were well-known at the time of the publication.

Equally condemning is the fact that the perceptron can actually model non-monotonic functions if we simply extend its definition and allow it to use non-monotonic activations functions, such as a sinusoid or a bell-shaped function. If we use multi-sigmoid functions then a perceptron can represent any Boolean function.

Irrespectively, the limitations of a single perceptron are irrelevant in the end. The real issue is in training multi-layer perceptrons (which are a specific form of artificial neural networks). Without any proof or even supporting evidence, the authors of the book claimed that such multi-layer perceptrons could not be effectively trained.

This is striking given that previous forms and variants of back-propagation had been published early in the 1960s. The underlying gradient-based methods to find local extrema of functions had been used in physics and calculus for centuries. Yet, the authors conveniently ignored those facts. As one might expect, their claims were eventually debunked. Mathematically, their entire book is ridiculous. It fails to make trivial mathematical observations; it projects limitations of logic onto perceptrons; it confuses global with local extrema and exact solutions with approximate ones; and it implies that we cannot use optimizations to approximate functions with multi-level parameterizations.

Let us examine those grand failures in more detail.

It is a trivial fact that a perceptron can model the logical functions "and", "or", and "not", the latter can be done simply by negating the weight of the corresponding input. It is equally trivial to infer that any logical circuit can be represented by multi-layer perceptrons of the same depth and with the same number of units as the number of gates in the circuit. This implies computational completeness and with the same time complexity as logical circuits. All this was well known at the time of the publication. The authors of the book were aware of it and they separately mentioned in a report in 1972.

There are two direct consequences of the above computational fact. First, if we are to make statements about the computational power of perceptrons and their time complexity, we must not limit their depth or their size. Second, and more importantly, all constraints about the structure and connectivity of multi-layer perceptrons are not intrinsic limitations of perceptrons but limitations of logic and thus of all of computing. For example, the global connectivity constraint that the authors proved in their book is a limitation of Boolean circuits. If there is no locally connected network of perceptrons to compute a given function, there cannot be a locally connected Boolean circuit that would compute the same function. (If there were such a circuit we could create an equivalent network of perceptrons with the same connectivity by replacing each gate in the circuit with the corresponding perceptron.)

Furthermore, and given that all Boolean functions can be converted in disjunctive (or conjunctive) normal form, three-layer perceptrons can model any Boolean function with three layers and as many hidden units as terms in the normal form. Of course, the normal form can have an exponential number of terms. Again that is not an intrinsic limitation of perceptrons but a fundamental a limitation of logic. In general, deep logical expressions cannot be represented by shallow ones with the same time complexity.

Despite the triviality of it, the authors failed to discuss or even notice any of the above. Instead, in a report in 1972, they made the following statement about three-layer perceptrons: "Virtually nothing is known about the computational capabilities of this latter kind of machine. We believe that it can do little more than can a low order perceptron."

The above is an astonishing claim. If we do not assume that the authors were as ignorant and incompetent as to fail to notice such trivial mathematical relationships, we can only conclude that their efforts were intentional and meant to mislead and bias the community against perceptrons -- and neural networks. The latter is furthermore supported by the fact that their claim is in direct contradiction with a statement they made that same year: "a universal computer could be built entirely out of linear threshold modules." It seems that the propagandists were lost in their own web of falsifications and contradictions.

There have been efforts to present the book and its criticism as a controversy somehow; or to shift responsibility from its authors to the field of artificial intelligence as a whole. The arguments in such reports are philosophical, sociological, qualitative, epistemological etc. They do not really examine the main issue that there was no science in the book. This is not surprising. The AI propaganda machine was on display many times before. It was once powerful when it attacked and attempted to ridicule H. Dreyfus's criticism of the field or when it attacked perceptrons and neural networks. Now, it is a negligible and defunct mechanism, obsolete, and irrelevant, too. In recent years, artificial intelligence has actually found a new role. It has attached itself to neural networks like a parasite, trying to draw life from the enormous success and magnitude of the neural enterprise.

After the revival of neural networks, even the authors of the anti-perceptron propaganda were quick to claim that they had not intended such a broad interpretation of the conclusions they reached in their 1969 publication. However, as the 1972 report indicates, their claim is contradicted by their own statements. Their intention was always to undermine the paradigm; and their latter argument is a desperate and conspicuous effort to hide the fact.

A more recent concern that rose with the proof of NP-completeness of neural network loading is equally misguided and misleading. The intentions of learning were never as absurd or impossible as to attempt to upset the hierarchy of complexity classes. Learning is primarily concerned with local extrema; and one of the main reasons is that global extrema are computationally expensive to find or verify.

Furthermore, there is a considerable degree of hypocrisy in those concerns. The same scientists who were so concerned about the complexity of neural network loading in the 1990s were not as alarmed when a similar result was shown for Bayesian networks or when planning was shown to be undecidable in the 1980s.

In the end, all of those theoretical limitations are practically irrelevant. All universal systems have similar constraints. Any system that is complete within a computation class must satisfy the complexity characteristics of the class. There is nothing new or different about neural networks. If we reject them because of such limitations, we may as well reject all of computing.

For similar reasons, there is not really any rationality in an argument that appeared in the early 2000s, against neural networks. Some researchers rejected neural networks or shied away from them because they found it hard to prove theorems about their performance and their characteristics. They chose to stick to areas where they could keep deriving theorems. For example, linear or logistic regression were popular among such researchers for many years because the simplicity of the models and their error surfaces allowed the researchers to prove theorems about convergence rates, global optima, confidence intervals etc. This is a state of affairs that demonstrates not only irrationality but also ignorance. Let us examine it in more detail.

There is fundamental trade-off between complexity and provability. Each system has an underlying *hypothesis space*, which is defined as the set of relations the system can potentially represent. As the complexity of the system grows, its hypothesis space grows and provability (the ability to prove theorems about the system) becomes harder or impossible.

Kurt Gödel's *incompleteness theorems* were published in 1931 and they were the first mathematical result in that direction. They demonstrated that any enumerable and consistent system of axioms cannot prove all true statements of basic arithmetic: there will always be true statements about the natural numbers that are not provable within the system.

In a letter to John von Neumann in 1931, Gödel furthermore described the *undefinability theorem,* which states that sufficiently expressive languages cannot represent their own semantics; in other words, any language capable of expressing the semantics of some other language L must have strictly greater expressive power than L. (The above result is often attributed to Alfred Tarski, who published a proof in 1936; Gödel never published a proof.) A direct consequence of the latter theorem is that the Church-Turing thesis implies that every Turing-complete computational framework has undecidable semantics.

Neural networks are practically universal (they can approximate any Borel-measurable function). As such their semantics are hard or intractable. Proving theorems about them would probably be hard (most likely as hard as proving theorems about natural numbers). However, if we follow the bias of researchers who rejected neural networks because of provability limitations, we should equally reject natural numbers because of their incompleteness. And we should either reject all universal computation frameworks (because of their intractable semantics) or reject the Church-Turing thesis. Of course, such rejections are irrational, baseless, and nihilistic (they permit only toys and trivial frameworks). Metaphorically, they are as absurd as an animal that chooses not to jump and not to run when trying to evade a predator because they cannot tell in advance precisely where they will land. Not surprisingly, such animals and researches share a common fate: extinction.

Ironically or hypocritically, the same researchers who rejected neural networks on the above grounds were not equally dismissive of the software industry. There is no complex software product that is provable. There are hardly any large software components that are logically verifiable or certainly free of glitches. We can never be certain about those things because software is a universal computation framework. There is a fundamental and critical factor behind those facts. Both nature and humanity have opted for complexity, not provability. The latter is a desirable property but it is often a luxury with a prohibitively high price.

Now, let us return to the 1969 anti-perceptron book. At this point, it should be clear that there was not any merit in it. Yet, it was hailed as a breakthrough by the artificial intelligence community. And one of the authors was given the Turing award in computer science. One might wonder about what forces, interests and considerations led a community of scientists not only accept but also celebrate such triviality enveloped with unsupported, misguided, and false claims.

We can answer the above question if we follow the money. The book spearheaded an effort to divert funding from neural networks into artificial intelligence. Various prominent figures in the latter field used their influence and power to that effect. Those efforts, combined with some hype in neural network research as well as the premature death of Rosenblatt, the inventor of the perceptron, led to a complete drainage of funding. Neural network researchers across the US were told by funding agencies to prepare for "very dry years". For more than fifteen years, there was hardly any neural network research within computer science in the US. Some research survived under neuroscience in medical or psychology departments but it was primarily about the structure and the function of the brain rather than the computational aspects of neural networks. There was some research in Europe and Japan but, again, it was not in computer science. Hopfield, for example, was a physicist. From 1969 to 1986, the field of neural networks experienced diminished growth because there was hardly any funding for it.

In short, "Perceptrons: an introduction to computational geometry" was merely a piece of propaganda that was disguised as science. Its main goal and only effect was to undermine connectionist paradigms and divert funding to artificial intelligence. The members of the latter field hastily declared the propaganda to be a scientific breakthrough. Motivations behind such indiscretions could vary. Some people were probably neither knowledgeable nor astute enough to comprehend the forces at play. Others may have felt validated in their beliefs and they did not bother to examine the facts. And some may have been simply corrupt. Whatever the motivations, this was a contemptible act. In any field that upholds fundamental scientific tenets, the authors of such propaganda would lose all credibility and likely their academic positions. They would certainly not be presented with scientific awards. The purpose of science is not to pretend, obscure, and misguide but rather to elucidate, predict, and confirm. It should be our path to truth, not a path to fallacies and deceptions.

Now, let us follow the money further. Where exactly did it go? It went into expert systems, knowledge based systems, logic systems, rule based systems, and all sorts of systems that had one thing in common. They could not scale. They could not handle real data. They were toys that operated well in highly simplified worlds but failed when they had to deal with the complexities, contingencies, and variability of the real world. Artificial intelligence researchers even coined a term for the problem. They called it the *frame problem.*

In the meantime, books were written like the "Rise of the expert company" that predicted a world run by expert systems. Those systems would write their own code, solve engineering problems, design computers, prove theorems, discover minerals and oil, travel in space, solve various medical problems, and perform all sorts of tasks where human expert knowledge was required. One of the projects aimed to encode all human knowledge in a knowledge base and the proponent of the project claimed that intelligence would emerge from such vast knowledge. It makes us wonder whether they also believed that genies could emerge from big bottles.

There was no science or rigor in any of the above. There was no mathematical basis or any supporting evidence for the claims. It was all a constructivist fantasy. Artificial intelligence has always been as much alchemy as it is science. Yet, alchemy somehow prevailed for nearly two decades. The proponents not only convinced government agencies to fund their fantasies but they also managed to persuade venture capitalists, too. Those who believed them and invested in their projects and their startups only saw their investments evaporate. In terms of returns, the most successful expert system startup was one that was acquired by a government agency.

By the end of the 1980s, both the government and venture capitalists had become aware of the fallacies and the fantasy. Funding was dramatically reduced and artificial intelligence startups were effectively extinct. The artificial intelligence community coined a new term: *artificial intelligence winter* -- by analogy with nuclear winters. Yet, there was no open criticism or condemnation of the field but rather a tacit complicity about it. Some resorted to excuses such as limited knowledge, scale or computing power. After all, no one wanted to admit that they had collectively invested billions of research and entrepreneurial funds to a pipe dream.

The very term artificial intelligence indicates the unfortunate mentality and bias of the person who introduced it as well as the many other similarly-minded people in the field. As we shall explain in the next chapter, there is only one form of intelligence, rigorously defined through learning, statistics, and the hierarchy of computational complexity. The rest are premises that have no basis.

In 1986, the back-propagation algorithm was published. It was a gradient descent method to train arbitrary neural networks. Some considered it a novelty and a breakthrough. It certainly had a dramatic effect. It revived the field of neural networks. Yet, there was hardly anything novel in it. Previous forms and variants of the algorithm had been published throughout the 1960s and the 1970s. Using the derivative to find local optima of non-linear functions was a common and centuries-old technique in physics and calculus. The only difference was that the method was finally and officially admitted into computer science. Engineers, researchers, government agencies, and venture capitalists suddenly became aware of it. Before the publication, the artificial intelligence community, in all their glory, had convinced the computer science world that such a method could not exist.

The prejudice against neural networks continued beyond 1986. After all, institutional biases take decades to correct and they usually require widespread resignations or retirements, shifts in education, and new generations of scientists. However, back-propagation had altered the game forever. Neural networks began competing with artificial intelligence for funding that was already becoming increasingly scarce. Not surprisingly, the artificial intelligence community coined new terms. Neural networks were *connectionist artificial intelligence;* everything else was *symbolic artificial intelligence.*

It is unfortunate that many neural network researchers accepted the distinction and chose to participate in such a notorious field. It has been argued that this was primarily a reconciliatory act and a recognition that a considerable portion of artificial intelligence (such as robotics or natural language processing, for example) were more rigorous paradigms that clearly had a place in science. We believe that the acceptance was a result of lack of leadership in neural networks. It is because of the same lack of leadership that the field effectively never proclaimed the 1969 publication as propaganda and failed to call the misdirection and corruption in the field of artificial intelligence with its true name.

The advent of the Internet (a.k.a. the world wide web) in late 1980s and 1990s generated large amounts of data and brought the entire field of machine learning to the forefront of research and the industry. Artificial intelligence researchers migrated to the new lucrative field in massive numbers. And they brought their prejudice with them. Researchers from a number of other disciplines converged too, particularly statisticians. The field was diversified and neural networks were simply one more paradigm in it, if not a peripheral one. There was clearly a bias against it. After all, paradigms such as decision trees, Bayesian networks, hidden Markov models, or even logistic regression were easier to understand and they did not have any of the connectionist 'stigma'. (Let us temporarily ignore the fact that logistic regression is a specific and trivial neural network.)

Neural Information Processing Systems (NIPS) was a conference that started in 1987 (proposed in 1986). It was meant to be an "interdisciplinary meeting for researchers exploring biological and artificial neural networks". Yet, by the mid-2000s, neural network publications were a small minority in the conference. NIPS was no longer a neural network conference but an amalgam of fashionable new approaches that were strictly ephemeral (e.g. support vector machines) and the old prejudice.

The above is not surprising. It is actually the most adverse and lasting effect of institutional bias. The prejudice against neural networks had created generations of computer scientists who hardly knew what a neural network was. In order to demonstrate and understand the magnitude of the ignorance, let us consider two examples.

One of the leading members of the Imagenet project recently described the winning neural network entry of 2012 as follows: "it was something that was called a convolutional neural network." The wording here is significant. The researcher did not say that it was a convolutional neural network, or a CNN, which is a commonly used acronym, because, we believe, they were aware that most computer scientists would not know or have not heard the term. The latter is an easily verifiable fact to this day and despite the extraordinary success of neural networks. Given that a convolutional neural network is the neural equivalent of an iteration (a.k.a. a loop), such level of ignorance is astonishing. It is equivalent to a computer scientist who have never heard anything about the concept of a for-loop.

Let us consider a second example. In on-line advertising, deep neural networks consistently provide dramatic gains. Companies that switch to them observe significant increases of their advertising revenue. This is becoming common knowledge but adoption is slow primarily because it is hard to find people with the right set of skills. After all, why would an average computer scientist who graduated a decade ago bother to take classes, if they were any, and learn anything about something that is called a neural network? Simplistic models such as logistic regression are more commonly used in on-line advertising. Because of their obvious limitations, desperate measures have been taken such as adding second order terms.

Those models have a fancy name: *factorization machines*. The name gives the impression of sophistication while, in reality, it is a trivial construction. Of course, none of those models can even compare with deep neural networks. Many logistic regression researchers and engineers have begun to realize the fact and they have tried to educate themselves in neural networks. Others choose to delude themselves and seek to invent features that would somehow keep logistic regression models afloat. One such researcher recently asked the following question: "When would logistic regression be better than neural networks?"

We must pause for a moment here and wonder at not only the level of ignorance but also the degree of absurdity in the question. It is like asking when a sparrow would be mightier than birds. The sparrow is not mighty on the first place; but even if it were, it could not possibly be mightier than birds because it is a bird. The same is true for logistic regression. It is a rudimentary model that cannot compare with generic neural networks. And even if it could, it would never be better because it is a neural network -- albeit one with no hidden units, and with a specific activation function, and, originally, a specific loss function.

Most likely, the researcher meant to ask a different question but phrased it in an unfortunate manner. When would a linear model be expected to be better than a nonlinear one? The answer to that question is trivial. The problem must be 'mostly' linearly separable. (The exact condition is that linear separability should be probably approximately correct.) However, such problems are very easy and rarely ever occur in practice. If a human derives a set of features that make a problem linearly separable, the solution is not the model but the features. Unfortunately, human engineered features is clearly a constructivist solution. If we impose linear separability as a requirement, the problem becomes unnecessarily hard. There is not really any real domain where humans have managed to find such features. The whole idea is yet another constructivist fantasy.

There is no doubt that each individual is responsible for their own state of mind and the knowledge and the skills they choose to acquire. However, we must notice that researchers like the one described above are also victims of an educational bias in computer science that is a direct effect of the prejudice against neural networks.

This is indeed the most lasting and harmful effect of institutional bias. Given the recent success of neural networks and their empirically demonstrated power, various computer science departments have hurried to hire neural network faculty and introduce related material in their curriculum. Even schools that were centers of symbolic artificial intelligence have changed. However, it will take at least one or two generations before we have a large fraction of appropriately educated graduates. Most likely, there will not be sufficient numbers of such graduates to support the industry. Neural network research and applications are already growing dramatically and their pace will only accelerate in the coming years. The prejudice has led us to a state where the education system has fallen behind and it must somehow catch up.

The prejudice and the consequent deficits in research and education have led the entire field of computer science in a constructivist predicament. Initially, constructivist solutions for software engineering were appealing and successful. Remarkable products like the C programming language and the Unix operating system are testaments to the fact. However, a transition ought to have taken place as the structural complexity of systems increased. Learning and self-organizing systems had to be researched and developed to replace or at least reduce the burden of human engineered solutions. That transition never took place. The prejudice effectively deprived us of the only learning paradigm that could have kept pace with the exuberance in computer science and the great demand for increasingly more complex systems. Constructivism became the only option for carrying the burden of complexity. The education deficit actually led many computer scientists erroneously assume that there was no other way. This is not surprising. Education deficits can have severe adverse consequences.

The same prejudice and deficit provide an answer to the first question of the first exhibit: the slow progress in the neural network paradigm. Neural network research advanced so slowly because it was denied funding and representation in computer science departments. Intelligent and talented students who could have made a difference were simply redirected to other areas. Some never heard of neural networks, their fundamental nature, and their importance for computing and intelligence.

The prejudice also affected neural network researchers and tried their convictions. When the world turns against a minority, the minority usually does not thrive, or even survive. Fortunately for science and humanity, neural networks have survived. They have succeeded against the prejudice and all the odds and they have now achieved the dominant role that is warranted by their mathematical foundations and scientific rigor. This is perhaps the greatest testament to their power, as well as the vision and persistence of those of us who unwaveringly supported the field throughout the years.

Finally, let us consider the second question of the first exhibit: Why does the neural enterprise takes place now? Various myths have been circulated in on-line forums and discussions. Some claim that the neural enterprise takes place now because of increased computing power. Others argue about large amounts of data or technological advances that were not previously available. None of those claims is accurate.

Neural networks do require greater computational resources for their training. However, in most cases, training takes place off-line; and long off-line training times of many days or weeks are tolerable. In general, a user of a handwriting or speech recognition system that uses neural networks would not experience any of the training times. The only delay they see is the time to run the network through the input they provide. There was clearly enough computing power to run sufficiently large neural networks for many applications at least two decades ago.

**Figure 3.** HP Compaq tablet PC.
(Source: wikipedia.org. By Janto Dreijer -- Own work. Public domain, via Wikimedia Commons.)

For example, the tablet PC group at Microsoft used a time-delay neural network for handwriting recognition as early as 2002. The requirements were that the network should have a maximum 3 millisecond runtime for each handwriting sample. It was part of a more complex architecture that used multiple neural networks and many other components such as a dynamic programming component and a language model. The whole system was running locally on a tablet -- which was not a very fast computer -- and it was real-time. Its accuracy was well beyond state-of-the-art at the time.

The reason that companies like Microsoft used neural networks earlier had nothing to do with computing power. Microsoft was not biased against neural networks and used the best available model for each application.

Many current state-of-the-art neural architectures for natural language processing only take minutes to train with today CPUs. If we apply Moore's law backwards, we can easily see that we could have trained such networks in few days at least 15 years ago. And if we used GPUs we could have trained them as early as 1999 when GPUs were introduced by Nvidia.

Computing power did play a role in the end. The bias against neural networks was so widespread that we had to reach a point where large neural networks could be trained by graduate students or researchers with limited academic resources. It was then inevitable that some of them would use the right architectures, submit their results, and win one competition after another. And when they did, computer science suddenly became aware of its prejudice and its fallacy.

The computing power argument is currently popular because it takes the blame from people and places it on machines, implying that it was not us or our biases that hindered progress. It was computers and their limited computing power.

The data argument might seem more plausible but, ultimately, it is incorrect. If we did have the technology and the computing power and the only missing piece of the puzzle were the data, why did we not start collecting them earlier? Projects like Imagenet should have started in the 1980s if not earlier. In certain domains like speech recognition, the size of data sets did not increase significantly in recent years. If sufficient data were the main issue and the amount of data did not increase significantly, why did the speech recognition community switch to neural networks now and not earlier? The truth is that big data sets have been available since the emergence of the Internet in the 1990s. If the amount of data was the issue, neural networks would have dominated machine learning on the Internet before the beginning of this century.

Finally, the argument about technological advances is incorrect too. The architectures we currently use for neural networks date back to the 1980s and the 1990s. Solutions for deep networks were published in the 1990s. The last component was the embeddings and those were published in 2003. If technology was the bottleneck, why was the neural enterprise delayed for one more decade and it did not take off in 2003?

In fact, both the first and the second question of the first exhibit trace back to the same source and admit similar answers. The neural enterprise takes place now because the prejudice against neural networks has been dispelled and has been replaced by firm convictions of their potential and the changes that they are to bring about to the world. The same prejudice was the main force that kept computer science from making reasonable or rapid progress in neural networks and truly non-artificial intelligence. When that barrier was removed, progress rates exploded, revolutions, tsunamis and electricities were suddenly unleashed to the world.

# 4. Learning versus intelligence

The importance of learning cannot be overestimated. Let us examine some facts to understand why.

Heraclitus (circa 535 – 475 BC) was a Greek philosopher who propounded that ever-present change is the essence of the universe. His phrase "πάντα ῥεῖ" (panta rhei) "everything flows" concisely describes his philosophy. A similar quotation from Heraclitus appears in Plato's dialogue *Cratylus*: "all entities move and nothing stays still." It is striking that such a realization of the nature of the universe appeared so early.

More than 2000 years later, the German mathematician and philosopher Gottfried Leibniz (1646 – 1716) considered the question of a universal formal language that could unequivocally describe everything in the universe. Like Heraclitus, Leibniz realized the essential role of change and thus he set out to produce a formalism that could describe change in a quantitative way. The result was the discovery of differential and integral calculus, which is one of the most influential mathematical theories of all time. There is hardly any paradigm in physics that does not use differential equations. The theory set the stage for modern science and technology.

This is not coincidental. Change is a fundamental and essential property of the universe. When change is persistently made so that a cost function is optimized, then the change is *learning*. Biologists often use the term *adaptation* to describe similar phenomena.

Learning is thus as fundamental as change. There cannot be life without learning. And there cannot be intelligence either. Entities that cannot adapt to changes in their environment cannot survive. They cannot and should not be treated as intelligent no matter how extensive their knowledge is. An encyclopedia, for example, cannot be treated as intelligent.

We do not have to resort to qualitative arguments. Learning is so fundamental that it can be used to define intelligence formally. For that purpose, we will use the concept of *probably approximately correct learning* (PAC-learning).

PAC-learning was proposed in 1984 as a way to describe learning that could generate systems of arbitrarily low error with arbitrarily high probability. We describe a variant below that takes into account the time complexity of the underlying problem and thus respects the hierarchy of computational complexity.

Assume a learning system $L$ and a relation $R$ that we attempt to learn through $L$. Let $Err(L, A, R)$ denote the expected error of an approximation $A$ of $R$ produced by $L$ and $T(R)$ be the time complexity of $R$ (or the class of $R$, if $R$ is an instance of a broader class). We define that $R$ is *efficiently PAC-learnable* by $L$ if and only if for all $\delta$ and $\varepsilon$ such that $0 < \delta, \varepsilon < 1$ there is a polynomial $p(1/\delta, 1/\varepsilon)$ such that

    a.  the time complexity of $L$ generating $A$ is $O(p(1/\delta, 1/\varepsilon) + T(R))$

    b.  the time complexity of membership in $A$ is $T(R)$, and

    c.  the probability that $Err(L, A, R) > \varepsilon$ is less than $\delta$

(The *big-O* notation is defined as follows: given two real functions $f$ and $g$, it is $f = O(g)$ if and only if there exist constants $c$ and $a$ such that $|f(x)| \leq c|g(x)|$, for all $x \geq a$.)

Now we can define intelligence. A learning system $L$ is *intelligent* if and only if all Turing-decidable relations are efficiently PAC-learnable by $L$.

(Note that we can extend the above definition to Turing-computable relations imposing the bound only for samples for which a Turing machine terminates -- for there cannot be a bound for all samples. However, that is equivalent to using a decidable restriction of the computable function instead of the whole function.)

The above definition implies that there is one and only one form of intelligence. Although we could create gradations of intelligence based on the degree of inefficiency of the approximation or the learner (including the degree of $p(1/\delta, 1/\varepsilon)$ when $R$ belongs to $P$, the class of polynomial time complexity), those are not different forms of intelligence but rather inefficient approximate versions of the one and only intelligence. Their only disadvantage is that they may take more time to solve the same problems.

On the other hand, a formal definition of intelligence without using learning is an exercise in futility. The best we can hope for are tests like the Turing test. Such tests are not a definition of intelligence by any means but rather methods to detect intelligence that is indistinguishable from a preexisting manifestation. In the case of the Turing test, both the distinguishing and the preexisting intelligence are human intelligence.

Similarly, the many definitions of intelligence that have appeared within psychology are primarily phenomenological or psychometric. They define intelligence as a set of demonstrable capabilities such as reasoning, planning, learning, perception, comprehension of complex ideas and phenomena, problem solving, creativity, self-awareness etc. An entity or agent must have all of those capabilities in order to be intelligent. However, those definitions focus on effects and they do not define the mathematics, the source, or the cause behind the effects. Most importantly, they fail to notice that the various capabilities are merely applications and instances of universal learning. The latter is the enabling mechanism of intelligence and the core of our definition.

In the end, intelligence is a phenomenon that emerges from learning and thus from change. That is the main reason why the field of artificial intelligence has been such a broad failure. It failed to realize and admit the paramount role of change and learning. In a private conversation, a prominent figure of artificial intelligence claimed that learning was "merely an annotation of intelligence." There has not been any evidence to support such a claim. The only intelligence that we know is biological intelligence and it is based on learning. There are no mathematical theories that suggest that we can factor out change and thus learning. And yet many artificial intelligence researchers were somehow certain that learning was irrelevant or insignificant and they largely ignored it. There was no basis for their assumptions.

There is nothing artificial about the emerging digital intelligence either. It is long overdue that we retire the term "artificial intelligence" as a reference to it not only because of its presumptive nature but also because it is misleading. If we assume that the adjective indicates "imitation" or "sham", the term implies that there are multiple types of intelligence and the new one is somehow inferior. And if we assume that "artificial" was intended to mean "humanly contrived" the term is misleading because learning is about autonomy rather than dependence on human engineering. Learning will eventually become fully autonomous. At its current state, it is partly dependent on human efforts to collect the data and define the architecture of the model and partly autonomous because the models are learned from data without human intervention. Of course, it is a long way to full autonomy. However, in science and especially in mathematics, we should not adopt terms that have an expiration date.

On the other hand, if we do we wish to distinguish between different manifestations of intelligence, a more appropriate way is to refer to their physical implementation. For example, human intelligence can be treated as an instance of *biological intelligence* while the emerging neural network intelligence can be indicated as *computer intelligence* or *digital intelligence* (assuming that computers will remain digital). For the rest of this book, we will use the latter term except when we wish to refer to the existing field of artificial intelligence.

We shall note, as we close this chapter, that its title is rather meaningless. Intelligence is a phenomenon and learning is the enabling mechanism and the foundation of it. We cannot compare the two. Yet, the issue arises in discussions sometimes. We adopted it in order to indicate that abstract or qualitative arguments can occasionally promulgate distractions and confusion

# 5. The dawn of the neural age

The neural enterprise is currently at an early stage. It started slowly about five years ago and it will keep expanding and growing for at least 40 to 50 more years. The aggregate effect on art, science, and society is hard to imagine. There is nothing in human history so far that can compare with it. There is no economic or other factor that will not be dwarfed by it. Let us consider some examples so that we can begin to understand the magnitude better.

Autonomous vehicles is one of the first commercial applications of neural networks. It has been estimated that use of autonomous cars "could eliminate 90% of all auto accidents in the U.S., prevent up to $190 billion in damages and health-costs annually and save thousands of lives" and that it could "free up to 50 minutes per day for average consumers". Google's valuation is estimated to have already increased by about $140 billion because of their early and visionary investment in autonomous vehicles. It is furthermore estimated that autonomous cars would amount to "$2 trillion a year in revenue and even more market cap" in the US alone. The total impact on the global economy will be even more massive. Car ownership will be largely replaced with transportation as a service, except perhaps in rural or remote areas. People will simply call an autonomous vehicle whenever they need transportation. There will be fewer cars and less demand for parking space in cities. Driving skills will become rare and unnecessary. Transportation of goods will be faster, safer, and cheaper. Algorithmic optimized traffic will utilize roads and transportation infrastructure better. Insurance standards will have to change. Even real estate values will be affected.

# Chapter 5. The dawn of the neural age

**Figure 4.** Autonomous automobile.
(Source: thespeedbarn.com)

As a result, a number of major automobile manufactures have started their own autonomous vehicle programs or have invested in related start-ups. Valuations have been sky-rocketing and they are only going to rise further.

The above numbers are indicative. Autonomous vehicles is only one application of neural networks and yet the numbers are impressive. In the course of the next 30 to 40 years, there will literally be hundreds of such applications, their aggregate effect on the economy and society will be stupendous.

We will examine the social effects in the next chapter. Let us now consider some skepticism.

There is indeed skepticism about neural networks and more often among artificial intelligence researchers or proponents of alternative learning paradigms. Some claim that artificial intelligence focused on the real problems and it was the only true effort to generate intelligence. They furthermore claim that the new enterprise is as much hype as artificial intelligence was in the 1980s and it cannot have a better fate. The motivations behind their arguments are unclear. There is certainly bias and sometimes bitterness but skepticism cannot be dismissed based on such terms. Neural networks and the neural enterprise are not free of hype -- or understatements. The future is hard to predict and many projects and startups will have premature or unrealistic goals. Not all neural ventures will be a success. On the other hand, as the numbers about autonomous vehicles indicate, neural networks have already reached a highly coveted state and have had an impact that indisputably distinguishes them from the artificial intelligence fantasies of the past as well as the rest of learning paradigms. Success can create envy sometimes or skepticism.

Natural language understanding with neural networks is a good example of both hype and understatements. Overall the area will experience high growth in the next decade. Its applications in on-line advertising have already generated great gains. The domain is currently shifting and companies that do not adapt will not survive. Similar applications in finance and algorithmic trading are obvious but have not been implemented on a broad scale, yet. Banks have started deploying conversational bots to assist clients with their transactions; but this is only a first step. Natural language processing has already been used in algorithmic trading but the systems are not as sophisticated as they could be. In the end, the shift will be dramatic. Of course, understanding of human language by neural networks is not anywhere near human levels at this point. A human trader or analyst has a better understanding of the things they read. However, neural networks can process hundreds of documents per second even when they run on a single CPU. They can aggregate information from multiple sources such as news sites, scientific articles, quarterly reports or even employee reviews on sites like glassdoor.com; and they can operate 24 hours a day, 7 days a week across different stock markets. They will win the competition against humans by the sheer volume of the information they aggregate and the speed of their processes.

Eventually, neural networks will be trained so that they encode the financial state of the world in extensive hidden layers of multi-million units. The level of detail and the amount of information that will be stored in such states is hard to comprehend or even imagine. The networks will then learn to map their state to short and long term predictions about individual stocks, funds, indexes, and the overall market. Most of the existing analytics will become obsolete and virtually useless.

There are many other areas that are affected by the increasing sophistication of natural language understanding. For example, IBM's Watson can offer virtually instant legal advice while bots are available to challenge parking tickets or to negotiate bills. News-writing bots have started to emerge. The Washington Post currently uses Heliograf to write news articles.

On the other hand, there is considerable degree of hype about certain areas of natural language understanding. Conversational bots is an example. Although, domain specific bots can be quite effective and will probably be successful, generic bots that are supposed to handle the entire range of human conversations are currently not ready for consumer or commercial applications. Startups that attempt to build such generic bots or bot architectures will struggle in the coming years and they will either fail or be acquired. Api.ai is such an acquisition example.

The successes of the neural enterprise are already as numerous and broad as to dispel doubt and refute skepticism. Companies like Nvidia that foresaw the paradigm shift and provided hardware (GPUs) that could train and run neural

**Figure 5.** Tensor Processing Unit.
(Source: cloudplatform.googleblog.com.)

networks fast enjoyed dramatic increases in their valuation (200% in the last 12 months, 750% in the last 24 months from July 25, 2017). Early in 2017, Google announced a custom chip called Tensor Processing Unit (TPU) to support its Tensor flow platform for neural networks and machine learning in general. Later in the year, they also announced a cloud version called cloud TPU. The industry clearly understands that neural networks have become as important as to drive the design of hardware. And yet, this is only a prelude, the beginning of the enterprise. The bulk of it is still to come.

Deep neural networks have enabled rapid progress in computer vision in recent years. There are many applications such as image recognition, visual search, unconstrained face recognition, image and video captioning, and, of course, robotics. The combination of advanced robotics and 3D printing will fundamentally alter construction and manufacturing in the coming years. Cheap labor will become almost irrelevant. Cheap energy will become the primary limiting factor of manufacturing and facilities will move around the world to regions where affordable and renewable energy such as wind or solar is more easily available.

Agriculture will also be affected by affordable autonomous vehicles and robots. Farming with robots is now becoming a reality. Autonomous tractors and drones are used for spraying fields with increased accuracy and efficiency. Robots perform traditional farming tasks such as sowing or harvesting. Companies like Deepfield Robotics provide such tools. The increased productivity and the reduced costs, especially as hardware prices decrease, will reduce the cost of food items with potentially great effects on inflation and economies around the world.

**Figure 6.** Robotics for agriculture.
(Source: Deepfield Robotics.)

System security and fraud detection are areas that will benefit and improve significantly through neural networks. Operating systems will gradually be replaced by deep neural networks. Within few decades, it will be virtually impossible to find a sophisticated device that will be controlled by human engineered software.

Intelligence gathering, defense and weapons systems are areas that will experience dramatics shifts in the coming year. Unmanned combat aerial vehicles already appear on the decks of aircraft carriers. State of the art systems outperform experienced human pilots. Deployment of large sensor arrays are currently under investigation. IBM and the US Air Force Research Laboratory have announced their collaboration for a neural network system of 64 million neurons and 16 billion connections. In the end, combat vehicles, drones, and aircraft will be driven by large neural networks and will be fully autonomous. They will be able to perform various missions and they will significantly reduce the size of the military (in terms of humans) and the loss of human life.

Inevitably, art will be affected by neural networks, too. Currently there are neural networks that compose and play music as well as networks that imitate the style of various paintings. In the latter, the networks are able to separate content from style of paintings and then combine the style with arbitrary visual content. This is only the beginning. Within the next few decades, sophisticated networks will be developed that understand a wide range of aesthetics, style, and harmony and will compose their own. They will not merely imitate. They will create new art -- and at rates that are humanly impossible.

The advent of the Internet created new standards and gradually re-defined a number of areas such as search and information retrieval, transactions and commerce, advertising, social networking, entertainment, and transportation. Many large companies emerged from it, such as Yahoo, Google, Amazon, eBay, PayPal, Facebook, LinkedIn, Netflix, and Uber. However, education has notably been left behind. The most successful

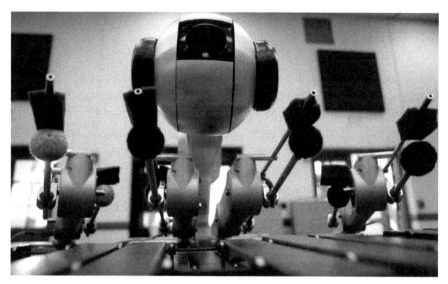

**Figure 7.** Georgia Tech's musical robot can compose and play its own original music.
(Source: Georgia Tech.)

company so far seems to be Khan Academy, which uses a crowd-sourcing model. Various universities offer their courses for free on-line. Wikipedia is a useful source of content but it is largely not pedagogical. These are important developments but they are only incremental. On the other hand, neural networks will bring a new wave of educational products that will redefine the sector.

The advent of the Internet created new standards and gradually re-defined a number of areas such as search and information retrieval, transactions and commerce, advertising, social networking, entertainment, and transportation. Many large companies emerged from it, such as Yahoo, Google, Amazon, eBay, PayPal, Facebook, LinkedIn, Netflix, and Uber. However, education has notably been left behind. The most successful company so far seems to be Khan Academy, which uses a crowd-sourcing model. Various universities offer their courses for free on-line. Wikipedia is a useful source of content but it is largely not pedagogical. These are important developments but they are only incremental. On the other hand, neural networks will bring a new wave of educational products that will redefine the sector.

Medicine and biology will greatly benefit from neural networks. The specific areas and applications are too many to list here and difficult to imagine in a comprehensive way. DNA research and detection of pathologies, autonomous diagnostic systems, and robotic surgery are three areas that we distinguish as potentially high-growth. DNA research in particular may experience an explosive growth. It is likely that within one or two decades, sophisticated neural networks will be trained and their understanding of DNA, as encoded in their hidden layers, will far exceed that of human experts. At three billion base pairs, the DNA is a structure that offers virtually unparalleled opportunities for neural networks. Human experts cannot possibly handle such long sequences and their understanding will always be at a very high level and rather qualitative.

The above list is not exhaustive by any means. The applications and the effects of neural networks will be widespread and fundamental. Some applications are impossible to imagine. The current rate of new results and important publications is so high that it is more than a full-time job to keep up with everything and only at a high level. It is a true genesis.

This is indeed the dawn of a new era.

# 6. The jeweled city on the horizon

Science is primarily about truth, validated theories, and verifiable facts. However, when we try to imagine the future, we can neither validate theories nor verify claims. There cannot be a method to distinguish potential facts from fiction because the facts of the future have not materialized yet. We may envision a "jeweled city on the horizon, spires rising in the night" per the words of N. Mailer, but those may turn out to be "diadems of electric" and "neon of signs". Inevitably, when we discuss the future, we cross the line that separates science from speculation and fiction.

On the other hand, if we focus only on verifiable facts we will rarely, if ever, be mistaken, but we will force a myopic horizon upon ourselves and we will entirely deprive ourselves of vision.

For the rest of this text, we will intentionally cross the above line in our effort to imagine the future and we will attempt to push our horizon all the way to the end of this century. Of course, the further we move from the present, the greater the uncertainty will be.

Let us return to the applications we mentioned in the previous chapter. Their timelines will probably vary because their underlying complexities and economic factors are different. For example, autonomous vehicles will most likely materialize and become widespread before autonomous defense systems or manufacturing. We anticipate that automatic fraud detection and autonomous vehicles will become the norm within one or two decades. Defense systems and military applications will become increasingly more sophisticated and they may achieve full or nearly full autonomy within the next thirty years.

# Chapter 6. The jeweled city on the horizon

Manufacturing, agriculture, and construction will probably take three to four decades to be fully automated.

The above may seem as remote predictions of the future and potential outcomes that have no immediate economic, social, or scientific effects. However, this is not the case. Let us understand why.

The time scale for full autonomy is not very informative and can be misleading. Most applications will take place gradually. For example, autonomous tractors and drones spraying fields as well as robotic systems operating in controlled greenhouses will take place much sooner and they will probably become widespread within one or two decades. Of course, a large number of farming jobs will not be replaced in the same time frame. Many farming jobs require high dexterity levels and the corresponding robotic systems will not be available or affordable in the next two decades.

On the other hand, the industry that will design and manufacture the corresponding machinery and intelligence will not suddenly appear. It is in an early stage now and it will gradually develop alongside with the neural enterprise. Jobs will be displaced as technology advances and costs are reduced. Within three to four decades, it is unlikely that there will be many economically viable jobs for humans in agriculture. Very specialized jobs might survive as well as jobs that handle environments that are adverse for robotics. However, the rest will be gone. The human body has not evolved for agricultural performance. We cannot possibly satisfy all the conditions. We are too tall to pick strawberries and too short to pick fruit from trees with minimal overhead. And we cannot work 24 hours a day, seven days a week. Once robotics reach the necessary levels of dexterity, the elimination of jobs will be rapid and dramatic.

The same issues and factors apply to manufacturing and construction. All those areas require comparable levels of robotic dexterity and sophistication. However, it is likely that manufacturing may advance faster because of the greater economic benefits. Robotic advances in manufacturing will probably transfer to construction and agriculture to some extent. In the end, the effect on employment will be similar. Within three to four decades, the majority of manufacturing, construction, and agriculture jobs will be eliminated; only a tiny minority might survive.

We can apply a similar analysis to many other major industry sectors such as mining, wholesale and retail trade, transportation and warehousing, financial activities, educational services, health care and social assistance, leisure and hospitality, and government. Within 40 or 50 years, most of those jobs will be eliminated. For some sectors (such as transportation and warehousing), there will hardly be any jobs for humans in the second half of the 21st century and possibly sooner.

On the other hand, the human population is not expected to decrease as dramatically in the above time scale. On the contrary, the human population of earth is currently estimated at 7.5 billion people and, according to the United Nations Population Division, it is expected to increase continuously and reach 10 billion by the year 2055 (see figure 8). This raises a question: what will all those people do, if more than half of the current human jobs are taken by neural networks and robots?

In general, the advantages of intelligent systems are just too many. For example, who would choose to use a human employee if they can deposit a check, renew their passports, take an exam, have an accurate medical diagnosis, or plan a vacation through a much faster, reliable, and always available conversational assistant? Even if the assistants fail sometimes, humans will only be used as a reserve service to handle the failures. And the number of failures is bound to decrease over

# Chapter 6. The jeweled city on the horizon

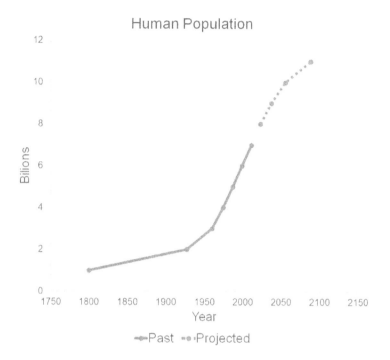

**Figure 8.** Human population on earth (current and projected).

time as the systems become more sophisticated and more intelligent and they learn from their own mistakes.

In the end, the neural enterprise will have major effects on the planet, humanity, and society. It will dramatically increase productivity and reduce the need for a human workforce. We will return to this issue and its social and political repercussions in the next chapter.

Let us now focus on the emerging digital intelligence so that we can understand it better. What form could it take? Are there any architectural predictions that we can make?

There are many anthropomorphic predictions that envision robots of various sizes and skills walking around and performing different types of tasks. Similarly, autonomous vehicles and devices are postulated. It is likely that those predictions will turn out to be true or partly true. However, we believe that the real and most powerful intelligence will not be in robots, vehicles, or devices. It will not be anthropomorphic either. Instead, it will be like a mycelium.

In Wikipedia, the *mycelium* is defined as "the vegetative part of a fungus or fungus-like bacterial colony, consisting of a mass of branching, thread-like hyphae." A mycelium can be a massive life form, the largest on record spans 2400 acres and it is 2200 years old. Mushrooms are merely the fruiting bodies of a mycelium and a minor part of the whole organism.

**Figure 9.** Fungal mycelium in petri dish on coffee grounds. (Source: wikipedia.com. By Tobi Kellner, Own work, CC BY-SA 3.0, https://commons.wikimedia.org/w/index.php?curid=18340817)

In a similar fashion, the *neurolium* will be a vast neural network and a form of intelligence that will exist on computer networks, span indefinite numbers of computers, and live eternally -- or at least as long as the network exists. Robots, vehicles, and various devices will merely be the 'fruiting bodies' of the neurolium.

Governments and large corporations will develop their own neurolia to monitor their processes, control their resources, manage their populations or employees, and manufacture and improve their products. They will quickly realize, however, that improving the neurolia themselves is their most important and strategic initiative. For example, an improved neurolium could give an advantage to a corporation against their competitors, or enable a financial institution to outperform others. Long before the end of the century, competition will solely be a battle of neurolia.

On the other hand, the most fascinating aspect of neurolia is not competition but rather cooperation. We humans can interact and learn from each other but the process is rather limited and slow. We cannot read each other's minds, aggregate our knowledge and experiences, or fuse our brains somehow. We can only communicate and process information about one another. Neurolia, however, if they choose to cooperate, they could share everything: data, experiences, knowledge, resources, components, robots and devices. And the aggregation could be done at any level, including individual units. Most likely, new aggregation methods will be discovered (by either humans or the neurolia themselves). The possibilities are endless and hard to imagine in a comprehensive way.

Irrespective of its form or the mode of operation, the importance of the new technology is gradually becoming common knowledge. Industrial and political leaders have already indicated the paramount and central role of the new technology. Several corporations have created specific organizations dedicated to the neural enterprise. Political leaders, such as the Canadian prime minister, have explicitly stated that their intention is to make their countries "world leaders" in this new arena. China has released a development plan with similar ambitions. While writing this text, the Russian President stated that "whoever becomes the leader in this sphere will become the ruler of the world" and that the new technology represents "the future, not only for Russia but for all humankind".

(Unfortunately, all of these leaders and corporations have adopted the term "artificial intelligence" to refer to the neural enterprise and the emerging digital intelligence. We can only hope that they will improve their terminology and abandon alchemical references as they understand the technology better.)

On the other hand, and if there is one and only one intelligence, as we claimed in section 4, one might question whether the digital intelligence can offer any advantage over biological intelligence. Is it truly new or is it merely old wine in new bottles?

If we examine the definition of chapter 4 more closely, we can see that there is a hidden constant in the big-O notation of condition a. Such constants can make a big difference. Perception is comparatively slow for humans, especially when the input is in the form of long sequences (e.g. text or a DNA molecule). For such tasks, the human constants are enormous. A person cannot possibly read millions of sentences or examine billions of bases in DNA. Neurolia will outperform humans on such tasks by orders of magnitude.

A second limitation in biological intelligence is the generic set of skills of individual organisms. For example, the ability of a human to appreciate true art or comprehend quantum physics does not really add anything to their ability to drive a vehicle. It is a fundamental fact that most of our intelligence is effectively useless for most of the tasks we do. This is a form of *cognitive locality* (in analogy to computational locality). Even for high-intellect tasks such as theorem proving, our abilities to process tactile, olfactory, or auditory information and thus our ability to appreciate a delicious meal or evocative music are practically irrelevant. (Theorem proving is more about reasoning, planning, vision, and motion.) Consequently, our vast neural resources are an equally vast waste for most of the tasks we perform.

A third disadvantage is the emotional nature of biological existence. Emotions like fear were essential for the survival of species in the wild. Yet, the same emotions are a liability for many tasks. A human can freeze in an emergency and miss the opportunity to take crucial actions that could prevent an accident or any other undesirable outcome.

Finally, there are gradations of intelligence that are expressed by the degree of the polynomial $p$ in the definition. It is not clear whether human intelligence is at the top of the scale or not.

On the other hand, there are tasks and areas of human endeavor that have little cognitive locality. Human intelligence and social behavior are often dependent on context and emotion as well as each individual's lifetime of experiences. Those experiences can be crucial for the development of sophisticated emotions and states of mind (such as empathy, dignity, or gratitude) and for the understanding of complex situations and psychological dynamics. It can be argued that human interoperability, synergy, and adaptability will be hard for computers to equal or emulate. It can furthermore be argued that a great deal of human intelligence is inherently social and cannot be abstracted away from society.

There is certainly truth behind those arguments. Not all human tasks will be equally hard or easy for neural networks; tasks with little cognitive locality will probably be harder. Intelligence has a social aspect the same way it has an environmental aspect because both society and the environment are among the greatest sources of training samples. If it is unreasonable (and mathematically challenging) to separate a learner from its learning methods and sources then it should be equally unreasonable to separate intelligence from society or the environment. However, in the end, all of those arguments are misleading because they fail to notice that the qualitative differences are reducible to a common basis, which is the core of all intelligence. None of us was born with the set of skills and behaviors we currently have. We learned them along the way. Every single human skill or behavior corresponds to a computational entity stored in our brains and learned from data that are fed into our brains. The complexity, cognitive locality, and computational cost of such skills and behaviors greatly affect the amount of required training data and neural resources. However, those are quantitative differences (of required data and neural circuitry). There are essential qualitative differences but those are phenomenological -- not foundational.

Let us consider a concrete example to help us understand the above argument.

Assume a team of humans with diverse backgrounds and skill sets working on a project with the goal to fulfill certain needs of an organization or a community. Furthermore, assume that a manager is to oversee the team and provide vision and leadership, create a timeline, resolve conflicts, support and enable the team members to do their work, work with them to find feasible solutions when perfect or desired solutions are out of reach etc. Now, if we are to hire such a manager, the most essential skill that they must have is prior experience in managing such a team. There is no other skill comparable to it. This raises a question: why is such prior experience so essential? The short answer is because we, humans, learn from such experiences. Our previous experience indicates that we have acquired the necessary traits and skills through our other experiences in life; but it also demonstrates that we know how to apply those in the context of managing a team.

# Chapter 6. The jeweled city on the horizon

Now, let us consider replacing our team manager with a sufficiently large neural network. There is currently no neural network that can equal human performance on such a task, but let us speculate. There is also no comparison between the efficacy of human learning and machine learning. There is no known machine learning method that can produce similar results with the same amount of training samples. If we are to train a neural network to replace the human manager, we will need millions, if not billions, of transcripts or recorded videos of human meetings, interactions, experiences etc. so that the network can develop hidden states that are rich enough to encode necessary attributes such as empathy, respect, understanding of human traits, team dynamics etc. We may need specific architectures that we can be developed through evolutionary methods or plain trial and error. The network will be enormous with current standards. It will probably take few more decades before we can train such networks. And their training times may span several years. However, those are primarily quantitative differences. Neural networks and training sets will reach the necessary size in due time; and they will be applied to various domains that now seem qualitatively different.

In short, there are many areas, such as learning efficacy, context, sophisticated emotions, interoperability etc. where biological intelligence excels. However, its most prominent advantage is its sheer magnitude. The human brain is a vast computing entity. It contains about 100 billion neurons, each having about 10 thousand connections on average and operating at a sub-millisecond range. That amounts to more than a million TFLOPs. (A TFLOP is a performance unit and it corresponds to a trillion floating point operations per second.) Our brains can easily dwarf the largest data center on earth and yet they occupy a space as big as our heads and they consume trivial amounts of energy compared to data centers. Hardware will advance, of course, but it is unlikely that it can compare with biological brains in the near future.

Consequently, it is likely that hybrid digital and biological systems will eventually emerge. Neural tissue or even whole brains developed in labs may be used to increase the computing power of neurolia. Digital implants could be used to enhance brains. There are startups that investigate the latter. Ethical issues may arise but the world will evolve, one way or another.

Of course, no one can predict the future. There is considerable uncertainty, especially when we try to imagine a fast advancing technological world many decades ahead. There are technologies (such as quantum computing) that have tremendous disruptive potential. There may be others that have not emerged yet. Those cannot been factored in our predictions. However, there is one certainty. Irrespective of hype, skepticism, predictions, or new technologies, the rate of progress will be rapid. By the third or fourth quarter of the 21st century, it will be a new world altogether. Humanity will no longer be the only dominant intelligence on earth.

# 7. The less traveled road

Let us now consider the social effects of the neural enterprise.

It has been argued that, in the past, technology displaced a large number of jobs but it created many new high-paying jobs. Given that the population of earth is constantly increasing, technology must create more jobs than those that are made obsolete in order to keep unemployment at its current levels. Adding to this the fact that globalization can easily shift jobs across the planet, population growth on some parts of the earth can affect unemployment globally.

Furthermore, we cannot possibly assume that technology will increasingly depend on humanity or that such a dependency will always exist. As technology advances and becomes more intelligent and sophisticated, it will need fewer and fewer people in order to operate. Constructivism cannot survive in the long term. Technology will eventually become fully autonomous.

There are two types or stages to such autonomy. The first is *operational autonomy* and it indicates the ability to operate autonomously without external intervention or assistance. The second is *structural autonomy* and it indicates the ability of the system to modify its structure, evolve on its own, and improve itself. *Full autonomy* includes both operational and structural autonomy.

For most domains and systems, operational autonomy will probably be achieved before structural autonomy. In the end, technology will converge to full autonomy one way or another. The transition has started with machine learning. The duration of the transition is uncertain at this point. It may take one more century before technology reaches full autonomy, but it will get there sooner or later. Dependence on humanity is a tentative arrangement and merely a step in a long process of augmenting and expanding learning and thus intelligence.

If we are to focus on a shorter term, such as the next few decades, we can certainly claim that neural enterprise will create many new lucrative jobs for people with the right set of skills. However, for every job that it creates, it will displace tens or hundreds more. Autonomous vehicles can provide a glimpse into the new reality. One in seven jobs in the U.S. is transportation-related. We cannot expect the neural enterprise, even as a whole, to create that many jobs.

The above, combined with the ever-increasing population of earth, can create unprecedented levels of poverty and unemployment across the planet. Over-populated nations that have enjoyed an economic boom in recent years primarily because of cheap labor will be the ones most dramatically affected. Poverty will rise and governments, societies, and even democracy will have to adapt to survive. Productivity and wealth will increase dramatically but only a small fraction of the population will benefit from it. Wealth concentration will grow at currently unseen levels and governments will have to apply radical measures, such as negative tax rates or a free universal living wage to stabilize society.

By the end of the 21st century, or long before it, the utility and even the right of the human race to exist in a multi-billion population will be questioned. Our superior biological intelligence across the species of planet earth and the technology we have developed has given us the power, the means, and the ability to grow and sustain the population at the current levels. We have assumed such a right ourselves without any regard to the burden it places on the planet and its ecosystem. In many ways, it is an irrational and selfish state of existence that cannot withstand scrutiny.

Furthermore, it can be argued that humanity is on a path to devastate the planet and its ecosystem. There have been five major extinction events in the last 500 million years on earth: the Ordovician, the Devonian, the Permian, the Triassic and the Cretaceous event. Paleontologists have claimed that only the Cretaceous was likely caused by an asteroid that hit the earth. The causes for the rest are unknown but climate change is consistently associated with them. The arguments and the evidence are compelling. Regardless, we seem to be in the midst of the sixth extinction event. Global warming is already affecting the planet. Extinctions are currently taking place at 100 to 1000 times the background rate, according to the U.N.'s Millennium Ecosystem Assessment. Many have adopted the term *anthropocene extinction* for the sixth event. The effects of climate change could, indeed, be catastrophic. And yet we have treated climate change with such levity, doubt, sensationalism, and unsupported optimism. If anything, humanity has proved to be a liability in managing the ecosystem. A new management will eventually take place and it will treat the planet more carefully and responsibly.

In the end, we believe, the digital intelligence will merge or co-exist with humanity and biological intelligence. Productivity and progress rates will reach astonishing levels. Pollution will be reduced or diminished. Decisions, policies, and legal frameworks will be driven more by science, and less by special interests, politics, or religion. Capitalism will change. Societies will adapt and populations will be reduced and kept at manageable levels. Economies and nations, as well as the entire planet and its ecosystem will become more stable.

On the other hand, the transition may prove to be difficult. Population reductions will not be easy. The strain on over-populated nations will be enormous. Without radical economic measures to support the least privileged, poverty and unemployment will expand dramatically. Strict immigration policies may apply for a number of decades. Extreme political forces may gain power or greater representation. It will take great political will and coordination of nations to make the transition least painful. Some nations or sections of society may be permanently left behind, their populations living in abject poverty. At the end, the transition can be anything from graceful to atrocious.

Regrettably, the precedent is unfavorable. If we are to judge by human history so far, it is unlikely that humanity will take the graceful and less traveled road. The words of Robert Frost, at the end of "The road not taken," may now admit a poignant and ominous interpretation.

I shall be telling this with a sigh

Somewhere ages and ages hence:

Two roads diverged in a wood, and I --

I took the one less traveled by,

And that has made all the difference

# Bibliography

References are listed in chronological order, web pages are at the end.

1. Plato. *Cratylus.* c. 360 BC. Available at: http://classics.mit.edu/Plato/cratylus.html
2. G. Leibniz. "Methodi tangentium inversae exempla." November 11, 1673. English translation in *The Early Mathematical Manuscripts of Leibniz.* Open Court Publishing, p. 93, 1920.
3. R. Frost. *Mountain Interval.* Henry Holt, 1916.
4. J. Child. *The Early Mathematical Manuscripts of Leibniz.* Open Court Publishing, 1920.
5. P. Dirac. *The Principles of Quantum Mechanics.* The Clarendon Press, 1930
6. K. Gödel. "Über formal unentscheidbare Sätze der Principia Mathematica und verwandter Systeme, I." Monatshefte für Mathematik und Physik, v. 38 n. 1, pp. 173–198, 1931
7. A. Tarski. "Der Wahrheitsbegriff in den formalisierten Sprachen." Studia Philosophica. 1: p. 261–405, 1936.
8. R. Fisher. "The Use of Multiple Measurements in Taxonomic Problems." *Annals of Eugenics,* 7 (2): 179–188, 1936.
9. A. Church. "An Unsolvable Problem of Elementary Number Theory." American Journal of Mathematics. 58 (2): 345, 1936
10. A. Turing. "On Computable Numbers, with an Application to the Entscheidungsproblem." Proceedings of the London Mathematical Society, 2, 42, pp. 230–265, 1937.

# Bibliography

11. F. Rosenblatt. "The Perceptron -- a perceiving and recognizing automaton." Report 85-460-1, Cornell Aeronautical Laboratory, 1957.
12. B. Widrow, M. Hoff. "Adaptive switching circuits." IRE WESCON Conv. Rec., pp. 96-104, 1960.
13. H. Kelley. "GradientfPal theory of optimal flight paths." *Ars Journal,* 30 (10): 947–954, 1960.
14. A. Bryson. "A gradient method for optimizing multi-stage allocation processes." In Proceedings of the Harvard Univ. Symposium on digital computers and their applications, 1961.
15. S. Dreyfus "The numerical solution of variational problems." *Journal of Mathematical Analysis and Applications,* 5(1), 30–45, 1962.
16. N. Nilsson. *Learning Machines: Foundations of Trainable Pattern-Classifying Systems.* New York: McGraw-Hill, 1965.
17. H. Dreyfus. "Alchemy and AI", RAND Corporation, 1965.
18. J. van Heijenoort. *From Frege to Gödel: A Source Book in Mathematical Logic, 1879-1931, 3rd ed.* Harvard University Press, Cambridge Mass., 1967.
19. D. Hubel, T. Wiesel. "Receptive fields and functional architecture of monkey striate cortex." *The Journal of Physiology,* 195 (1): 215–243, 1968.
20. M. Minsky, S. Papert. *Perceptrons: an introduction to computational geometry.* M.I.T. Press, Cambridge, Mass., 1969 1969.
21. S. Linnainmaa. "The representation of the cumulative rounding error of an algorithm as a Taylor expansion of the local rounding errors." Master's Thesis, Univ. Helsinki, 6–7. 1970.
22. M. Minsky, S. Papert. "Artificial intelligence progress report." MIT artificial intelligence memo no. 252, 1972. Available at: http://bitsavers.trailing-edge.com/pdf/mit/ai/aim/AIM-252.pdf

23. H. Dreyfus, Hubert. *What Computers Can't Do*. New York: MIT Press, 1972.
24. P. Werbos. "Beyond regression: New tools for prediction and analysis in the behavioral sciences." PhD thesis, Harvard University, 1974.
25. W. Little. "The existence of persistent states in the brain." *Math. Biosci.,* 19, 101-120, 1974.
26. K. Fukushima. "Neocognitron: A Self-organizing Neural Network Model for a Mechanism of Pattern Recognition Unaffected by Shift in Position." *Biological Cybernetics,* 36 (4): 193–202, 1980. Available at: http://www.cs.princeton.edu/courses/archive/spr08/cos598B/Readings/Fukushima1980.pdf
27. P. Werbos. "Applications of advances in nonlinear sensitivity analysis." *System modeling and optimization,* Springer. pp. 762–770, 1982. Available at: http://werbos.com/Neural/SensitivityIFIPSeptember1981.pdf
28. J. Hopfield. "Neural networks and physical systems with emergent collective computational abilities." Proceedings of the National Academy of Sciences of the USA, vol. 79 no. 8 pp. 2554–2558, 1982.
29. L. Valiant. "A theory of the learnable." *Communications of the ACM,* 27, 1984.
30. D. Rumelhart, G. Hinton, and R. Wiliams. "Chapter 8 : Learning Internal Representations by ErrorPropagation." In D. Rumelhart, J. McClelland. *Parallel Distributed Processing, Volume 1.* MIT Press. pp. 319–362, 1986.
31. D. Rumelhart, J. McClelland. *Parallel Distributed Processing, Volume 1.* MIT Press, 1986.
32. D. Rumelhart, J. McClelland. *Parallel Distributed Processing, Volume 2.* MIT Press, 1986.
33. H. Dreyfus, S. Dreyfus. *Mind over Machine: The Power of Human Intuition and Expertise in the Era of the Computer.* Oxford, U.K. Blackwell, 1986.

34. D. Chapman. "Planning for conjunctive goals." *Artificial Intelligence,* 32:333– 379, 1987

35. G. Cooper. "Probabilistic inference using belief networks is NP-hard." Technical Report KSL-87-37, Knowledge Systems Laboratory, Stanford University, Stanford, California, 1987.

36. R. Feynman, R. Leighton, and M. Sands. *The Feynman Lectures on Physics.* Addison Wesley, 1989. Available at: http://www.feynmanlectures.caltech.edu/III_01.html

37. G. Cybenko. "Approximations by superpositions of sigmoidal functions." *Mathematics of Control, Signals, and Systems,* 2 (4): 303–314, 1989.

38. J. Elman. "Finding Structure in Time." *Cognitive Science,* 14 (2): 179–211, 1990.

39. K. Hornik. "Approximation capabilities of multilayer feedforward networks." *Neural Networks,* 4 (2): 251–257, 1991.

40. J. Schmidhuber, "Learning complex, extended sequences using the principle of history compression." *Neural Computation,* 4 (2): 234–242, 1992.

41. J. Drakopoulos. "Multi-sigmoidal units and neural networks." In Third European Symposium on Artificial Neural Networks, 341-346, 1995.

42. M. Olazaran. "A sociological study of the official history of the perceptrons controversy". Social Studies of Science. 26: 611–659, 1996.

43. U. Neisser, G. Boodoo, T. Bouchard, A. Boykin, N. Brody, S. Ceci, D. Halpern, J. Loehlin, R. Perloff, R. Sternberg, S. Urbina. "Intelligence: Knowns and unknowns" *American Psychologist,* 51: 77–101, 1996.

44. S. Hochreiter, J. Schmidhuber. "Long short-term memory." *Neural Computation,* 9 (8): 1735–1780, 1997.

45. M. Jordan "Serial order: a parallel Distributed Processing Approach." Advances in Psychology. Neural-Network Models of Cognition. 121: 471–495, 1997.

46. Y. LeCun, L. Bottou, Y. Bengio; P. Haffner. "Gradient-based learning applied to document recognition." *Proceedings of the IEEE,* 86 (11): 2278–2324, 1998.
47. R. Duda, P. Hart, and D. Stork. *Pattern Classification, 2nd Ed.* Wiley-Interscience, 2001.
48. E. Raymond. *The cathedral and the bazaar: musings on Linux and Open Source by an accidental revolutionary.* O'Reilly. 2001
49. Y. Bengio, R. Ducharme, P. Vincent, and C. Jauvin. "A Neural Probabilistic Language Model." JMLR 3:1137–1155, 2003. Available at: http://jmlr.org/papers/volume3/bengio03a/bengio03a.pdf
50. P. Stamets. *Mycelium Running.* Ten Speed Press, 2005
51. S. Legg and M. Hutter. "A Collection of Definitions of Intelligence." Proceedings of the 2007 conference on Advances in Artificial General Intelligence, pp. 17-24, 2007.
52. H. Honour and J. Fleming. *A World History of Art. 7th ed.,* London: Laurence King Publishing, 2009.
53. R. Collobert, J. Weston, L. Bottou, M. Karlen, K. Kavukcuoglu, P. Kuksa. "Natural language processing (almost) from scratch." *Journal of Machine Learning Research,* pp. 2537, 2011
54. A. Krizhevsky, I. Sutskever, G. Hinton "ImageNet Classification with Deep Convolutional Neural Networks." NIPS, 2012.
55. Y. Bengio, A. Courville, P. Vincent "Representation Learning: A Review and New Perspectives." *IEEE Transactions on Pattern Analysis and Machine Intelligence,* 2013.
56. Y. Taigman, M., Yang, M. Ranzato, and L. Wolf. "Deepface: Closing the gap to human-level performance in face verification." Computer Vision and Pattern Recognition, 1701–1708, 2014.

57. "L. Deng and D. Yu". *Deep Learning: Methods and Applications.* NOW Publishers, 2014. Available at: https://www.microsoft.com/en-us/research/publication/deep-learning-methods-and-applications/

58. J. Schmidhuber. "Deep learning in neural networks: an overview." *Neural Networks,* 61: 85–117, 2015.

59. L. Gatys, A. Ecker, M. Bethge. "A neural algorithm of artistic style." *CoRR*, 2015. Available at: http://arxiv.org/abs/1508.06576

60. P. Ward, J Kirschvink. *A New History of Life.* Bloomsbury Press, 2015.

61. W. Xiong, J. Droppo, X. Huang, F. Seide, M. Seltzer, A. Stolcke, D. Yu, and G. Zweig. "Achieving human parity in conversational speech recognition." Microsoft Research, Technical Report MSR-TR-2016-71, 2016. Available at: https://arxiv.org/abs/1610.05256

62. I. Goodfellow, Y. Bengio, and A. Courville. *Deep Learning.* MIT Press, 2016. Available at: "http://www.deeplearningbook.org" ,

63. A. Graves, G. Wayne, M. Reynolds, T. Harley, I. Danihelka, A. Grabska-Barwińska, S. Colmenarejo, E. Grefenstette, T. Ramalho, J. Agapiou, A. Badia, K. Hermann, Y. Zwols, G. Ostrovski, A. Cain, H. King, C. Summerfield, P. Blunsom, K. Kavukcuoglu, and D. Hassabis. "Hybrid computing using a neural network with dynamic external memory." *Nature,* 538, pp. 471-476, 27 October 2016.

64. H. Cohen. "The Perceptron. Perceptual Mathematics and Neural Net History." Available at: http://harveycohen.net/image/perceptron.html

65. "Nvidia launches the world's first graphics processing unit: GeForce 256." 31 August 1999. Available at: http://www.nvidia.com/object/IO_20020111_5424.html

66. R. Butler. "Past mass extinction events linked to climate change." March 29, 2006. Available at:

https://news.mongabay.com/2006/03/past-mass-extinction-events-linked-to-climate-change/

67. "Meet Your New Lawyer, IBM Watson." August 24, 2014. Available at: http://prismlegal.com/meet-new-lawyer-ibm-watson/

68. N. Nilsson. "The Future of Work: Automation's Effect on Jobs -- This Time Is Different." Pacific Standard, 2015. Available at: https://psmag.com/economics/the-future-of-work-automations-effect-on-jobsthis-time-is-different

69. "Deep Genomics launches, uniting deep learning and genome biology." July 22, 2015. Available at: http://www.kurzweilai.net/deep-genomics-launches-uniting-deep-learning-and-genome-biology

70. "Deep Genomics." 2015 Available at: https://www.deepgenomics.com/

71. "Grail." 2016. Available at: https://grail.com/

72. U. Gollub. "Singularity university summit summary." Facebook. April 22, 2016. Available at: https://www.facebook.com/udo.gollub/posts/102079788 45381135

73. "Farming with robots." May 4, 2016 Available at: http://robohub.org/farming-with-robots/

74. "Deepfield Robotics." Available at: https://www.deepfield-connect.com/

75. "New AI takes down experienced human pilots in virtual dogfights." July 4, 2016. Available at: http://newatlas.com/ai-human-pilots-dog-fights/44107/

76. "Google supercharges machine learning tasks with TPU custom chip." 2016. Available at: https://cloudplatform.googleblog.com/2016/05/Google-supercharges-machine-learning-tasks-with-custom-chip.html

77. "Google acquires API.AI, a company helping developers build bots that aren't awful to talk to." September 19, 2016. Available at: https://techcrunch.com/2016/09/19/google-acquires-

api-ai-a-company-helping-developers-build-bots-that-arent-awful-to-talk-to/

78. "An introduction to deep learning." November 4, 2016. Available at: https://blog.algorithmia.com/introduction-to-deep-learning-2016/

79. "Nvidia teams with National Cancer Institute, U.S. Department of Energy to create AI platform for accelerating cancer research." November 14, 2016 Available at: http://nvidianews.nvidia.com/news/nvidia-teams-with-national-cancer-institute-u-s-department-of-energy-to-create-ai-platform-for-accelerating-cancer-research

80. "What news-writing bots mean for the future of journalism." February 17, 2017. Available at: https://www.wired.com/2017/02/robots-wrote-this-story/

81. "Trudeau looks to make Canada 'world leader' in AI research." March 30, 2017 Available at: https://phys.org/news/2017-03-trudeau-canada-world-leader-ai.html

82. "Google's second generation TPU chips takes machine learning processing to a new level." May 17, 2017. Available at: https://techcrunch.com/2017/05/17/google-announces-second-generation-of-tensor-processing-unit-chips/

83. "Neural Networks and Deep Learning." May 2017. Available at: http://neuralnetworksanddeeplearning.com/

84. "Four-armed marimba robot uses deep learning to compose its own music." June 14, 2017. Available at: http://spectrum.ieee.org/automaton/robotics/artificial-intelligence/four-armed-marimba-robot-uses-deep-learning-to-compose-its-own-music

85. "US Air Force buying IBM 64 million neuron computer." June 24, 2017. https://www.nextbigfuture.com/2017/06/us-air-force-buying-ibm-64-million-neuron-computer.html

86. "Deep-learning networks rival human vision." June 26, 2017 Available at: https://www.scientificamerican.com/article/deep-learning-networks-rival-human-vision1/
87. "Elon Musk: 'Robots will be able to do everything better than us'." July 17, 2017. Available at: http://www.cnbc.com/2017/07/17/elon-musk-robots-will-be-able-to-do-everything-better-than-us.html
88. "China aims to become world leader in AI, challenges US dominance." July 20, 2017. Available at: http://in.reuters.com/article/us-china-ai/china-aims-to-become-world-leader-in-ai-challenges-u-s-dominance-idINKBN1A5103
89. "Nvidia a buy on '4th wave of computing': Jefferies." July 25, 2017 http://www.investopedia.com/news/nvidia-buy-4th-wave-computing-jefferies/?lgl=rira-baseline-vertical
90. "Putin says country that becomes AI leader will rule the world; Elon Musk warns it will cause WW3." September 5, 2017. Available at: https://www.techspot.com/news/70850-putin-country-becomes-ai-leader-rule-world-elon.html
91. "Economic impact on transportation." Available at: https://www.rita.dot.gov/bts/programs/freight_transportation/html/transportation.html
92. "Composing music with recurrent neural networks." 2017. Available at: http://www.hexahedria.com/2015/08/03/composing-music-with-recurrent-neural-networks/
93. "AI painter." Available at: https://www.instapainting.com/ai-painter
94. "Mycelium." Available at: https://en.wikipedia.org/wiki/Mycelium
95. Object-oriented programming. Wikipedia. Available at: https://en.wikipedia.org/wiki/Object-oriented_programming

# Bibliography

96. Open-source model. Wikipedia. Available at:
    https://en.wikipedia.org/wiki/Open-source_model
97. "Codebases. Millions of lines of code." Available at:
    http://www.informationisbeautiful.net/visualizations/milli
    on-lines-of-code/

www.ingramcontent.com/pod-product-compliance
Lightning Source LLC
LaVergne TN
LVHW052309060326
832902LV00021B/3788